This book belongs to

....

To M and D, who through their selfless love
and unending encouragement have instilled values
in me that are my treasures today.

A Child's Book of Values

Lesley Wright

DK

A Dorling Kindersley Book

Dorling Kindersley

LONDON, NEW YORK, SYDNEY, DELHI, PARIS,
MUNICH, AND JOHANNESBURG

Project Editor Jane Yorke
Art Editor Jane Horne
Publishing Manager Sarah Phillips
Deputy Design Director Mark Richards
DTP Designers Megan Clayton and
Almudena Díaz
Production Silvia La Greca
Picture Research Angela Anderson
Jacket Design Karen Shooter
U.S. Editor Claudia Volkman

Photography Steve Gorton
Illustrations Nadine Wickenden,
Diana Catchpole, and Carrie Hill
Religious Consultant Jonathan Sharples

Published in the United States by
Dorling Kindersley Publishing, Inc.
95 Madison Avenue
New York, New York 10016

First American Edition, 2001
01 02 03 04 05 10 9 8 7 6 5 4 3 2

Copyright © 2001 Dorling Kindersley Limited

ISBN 0-7894-6518-3

Color reproduction by Colourscan, Singapore
Printed and bound in Italy by L.E.G.O.

See our complete catalog at
www.dk.com

Contents

Teach your children to choose the right path,
and when they are older, they will remain upon it.
Proverbs 22:6

Introduction

One of the greatest gifts we can give our children is a strong foundation of personal values based on God's teachings in Scripture. Not only does this protect our children from peer pressure and the shallowness so prevalent in today's culture, but it helps them develop into well-adjusted, productive, and caring individuals.

Defining values

Values can be defined as desirable qualities and attitudes that, when learned and practiced, develop character, integrity, and purpose. Values are more than just skills to acquire. True values are meant to be internalized, ultimately defining who we become. Christian values are firmly rooted in biblical truth – essentially they are the "fruit of the Spirit."

Teaching your child Christian values

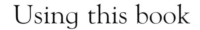

Helping children understand and practice Christian values – love, forgiveness, kindness, generosity, patience, gratefulness, responsibility, hard work, honesty, bravery, faithfulness, and joyfulness – is the goal of this book. As you explore with your child the meaning and practical applications of these twelve core Christian values, you will discover many ways of linking these values to your child's everyday experiences.

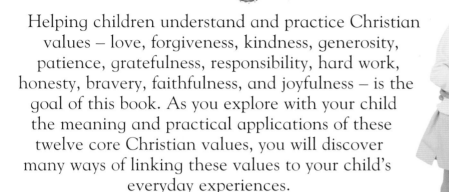

Using this book

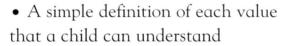

Each section of this book contains:

- A simple definition of each value that a child can understand
- Bible stories that illustrate the value
- Quotes from children
- Discussion points on practical ways to develop each value
- ☆ A key Bible verse denoted by the "star" symbol
- An informal prayer written by a child.

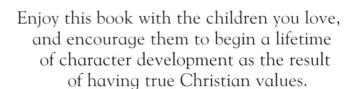

Enjoy this book with the children you love, and encourage them to begin a lifetime of character development as the result of having true Christian values.

Love

Love means caring so much for other people that it shows in the way you treat them. Love is more than a warm feeling; it is acting unselfishly for another's good. You can show love to your mom by giving her a big hug – or by doing the dishes for her without being asked. When you are full of love, you choose to act with kindness, patience, and forgiveness. You show your love by the things that you do and say.

God is love

We can love others because God first loved us. God showed us how much he loved us by sending Jesus into the world so we could have eternal life. When we look at God, we see what real love is. The Bible says, "Our love for [God] comes as a result of his loving us first."(1 John 4:19 TLB). Love is God's greatest gift – we don't have to earn it, and no one is left out!

8

Love doesn't end

Jesus told a story in *Luke 15:11-31* about a man who divided up his wealth between his two sons. The younger son took his share of the money and went looking for adventure. He spent all his money foolishly, and soon he was sad and hungry. He decided to return home, but was afraid of what his father might say. Imagine his surprise when his father ran toward him with loving, open arms. He was full of joy that his lost son had returned.

"I'm not jealous of our new baby, because I know Mom and Dad have enough love for us all."
Ellie

Love is not always easy

It's easy to love other people when they are kind and friendly. It's much harder when they are rude or selfish. But no matter how they act, you show your love for them by treating them kindly, fairly, and with understanding. Jesus even said that you should love your enemies! Follow Jesus' example by always finding ways to show love to others.

Love is loyal

Naomi was all alone because her husband and two sons had died. She wanted each of her daughters-in-law to find a new husband. But Ruth loved her mother-in-law so much that she chose to stay with Naomi. Ruth showed her love by being loyal to Naomi. To find out how God blessed both women because of their love for each other, read *Ruth 4:13-16*.

Love never gives up, never loses faith, is always hopeful, and endures through every circumstance.
Love will last forever.
1 Corinthians 13:7-8

Love is unselfish

Love sometimes means putting the needs of others before your own. This might mean helping your mom clean the house, rather than watching your favorite television program. God wants us to love others the same way we love ourselves. You can show your love for others in the small things you do for them every day. It will make a big difference!

Be loving!

How can I be loving at home?

- I can give my parents a hug and tell them I love them.
- I can spend time with my family and not always play computer games or watch TV.

How can I be loving to my friends?

- I can make sure that none of my friends feels lonely or left out.
- I can make my friends feel welcome when they come to my house.

How can I be loving toward others?

- I can share God's love with others through my kind words and actions.
- I can be understanding when someone is having a bad day.

Dear God,
Thank you for your precious love
that's as high as the sky,
As wide as the land,
and as deep as the ocean.
Help me to enjoy your love
and share it with other people.
It feels so good to know
that you will love me forever.
Amen.
Joshua

Forgiveness

Showing forgiveness is being willing to let go of the hurt and anger you feel when others wrong you. This might mean forgiving your sister for breaking your favorite toy, or hugging a friend who's sorry for letting you down. God wants us to follow his example. He is always ready to forgive you for your mistakes – all you have to do is ask him!

Forgive and forget

When others do something wrong to you, it's natural to feel angry or hurt. And it's not always easy to forgive them. If you don't feel very forgiving, try being kind to those who have wronged you. You could help them with a project, or give them your biggest smile. Soon you will find that you are able to forgive – and forget!

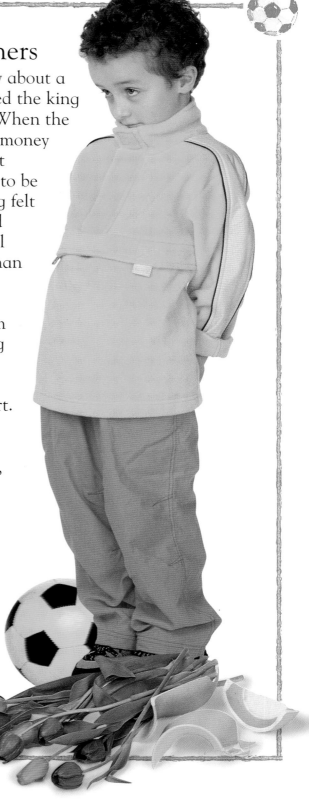

Forgive others

Jesus told a story about a servant who owed the king a lot of money. When the king wanted his money back, the servant begged the king to be patient. The king felt sorry for him and decided to cancel the debt. Then this same servant went to a man who owed him a small amount of money and demanded it back. When the man said he couldn't pay, the unforgiving servant had him arrested and locked up in jail! When the king heard what had happened, he was furious. Read *Matthew 18:23-35* to learn how the servant was punished for his unforgiving heart.

"When I ask God for forgiveness and mean it, he wipes away all the things I did wrong."
Charlie

Big or small, forgive it all

Being forgiven for something big is a wonderful feeling. When you're the one who needs to forgive, treat everyone the same way. Follow God's example and always be willing to forgive others, whether they've done a big wrong or a small one.

Family quarrel

Joseph was able to forgive his 11 brothers even though they had wanted to kill him and then had sold him as a slave. Many years later, Joseph became a powerful leader in Egypt. One day, the brothers came to Joseph during a terrible famine and asked him for food. Joseph forgave his brothers when he realized that they were sorry for what they had done. And Joseph showed his forgiveness by saving his brothers from starving and letting them come to live in Egypt. Read the whole story of how Joseph forgave his brothers in *Genesis 41-50*.

Be gentle and ready to forgive; never hold grudges.
Remember, the Lord forgave you,
so you must forgive others.
Colossians 3:13 TLB

Don't keep count

Just because you forgive someone once, doesn't mean you shouldn't do it again. Jesus tells us in *Luke 17:4* that we should always forgive those who are truly sorry, no matter how many times they ask. Forgiveness doesn't have a limit!

Be forgiving!

How can I show forgiveness to my family?
- I can give my brother a hug when he's sorry for fighting with me.
- I can stop arguing and apologize to my parents.

How can I show forgiveness to my friends?
- I can forgive a friend quickly and not hold a grudge.
- I can be kind and make it easy for others to say they're sorry.

How can I show forgiveness at school?
- I can forgive a classmate for being unkind, instead of telling the teacher.
- I can forget other people's mistakes and hope they forget mine.

Dear Jesus,
Thank you for your forgiveness.
Thank you for forgiving me
when I do something wrong.
Help me to forgive others
the way you forgive me.
Amen.
Isabelle

Kindness

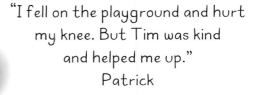

Showing kindness means being friendly and helpful toward others. Giving up your bus seat to an elderly person, sending a get-well card to a sick relative, or sharing your snack with a hungry friend are all ways to be kind. A few friendly words or a good deed can make all the difference to someone in your world.

"I fell on the playground and hurt my knee. But Tim was kind and helped me up."
Patrick

Be kind to others

A kind person cares about how others feel. Think before you tease someone or make fun of other people. How would you feel if friends treated you unfairly or left you out of their games? Jesus tells us to always treat others in the same way that we would like them to treat us. If you are kind to others, you are sure to have lots of friends who enjoy being with you.

Don't expect rewards

When Abraham was an old man, some tired and
hungry travelers passed by his camp in the desert.
Abraham kindly invited the strangers to rest in
the shade. He let them wash their weary
feet and gave them his finest food.
Abraham did not expect anything in
return, but God saw his kindness and
rewarded him in a special way. Read about
God's promise to Abraham in *Genesis 18*.

Kindness feels good

Every day you, too, can show
kindness to others in lots of ways.
Whether it's holding the door open
for someone carrying heavy bags, or
offering to help your brother with
his schoolwork, others will be
grateful for your kindness and
may learn to be kind too.

"When I carried some grocery bags
up the road for old Mrs. Harris,
she said I'd been a great help!"
Amy

Be a friend to everyone

Jesus explained how we should be kind to strangers in his story of the Good Samaritan. A Jewish man had been attacked and left for dead by some robbers. He was lying on the side of a lonely road. Two travelers came along but didn't want anything to do with him, so they passed by. Then a Samaritan, an enemy of the Jews, approached. He immediately felt sorry for the man and stopped to help. Find out how by reading *Luke 10:30-37*.

Since you have been chosen by God, and because of his deep love and concern for you, you should practice tenderhearted mercy and kindness to others.
Colossians 3:12 TLB

Be kind to animals

When Balaam's donkey refused to move, he beat it three times with a stick. Balaam was so cruel to his donkey that God allowed the animal to speak. Find out what the donkey said to his unkind owner in *Numbers 22:28*.

It's important to treat all God's creatures and their homes with respect. Be kind to animals, especially your pets. They can't tell you with words when they are hurt or hungry.

Be kind!

How can I be kind to my family?

- I can help Mom unpack the groceries.
- I can help Dad rake the leaves in the yard.

How can I be kind to my friends?

- I can hold my friend's hand when he's afraid.
- I can look after my friend's pet rabbit while she's on vacation.

How can I be kind to others?

- I can talk with an elderly neighbor who is lonely.
- I can offer to help if I see someone in trouble.

Dear God,
I started a new school today,
and everyone I met
was so kind and friendly.
Thank you for seeing that
I wasn't left out or lonely.
Help me to be kind
to others every day,
just like your son Jesus.
Amen.
Robert

Generosity

Showing generosity means giving to others and not expecting anything back in return. You can be generous by lending your bike to a friend who doesn't have one, buying a candy bar for your little brother, or spending time with a sick relative. Share with a generous heart and discover how happy it makes you and others feel.

Giving can be fun!

Some people find it very hard to give. They think if they give too much, they won't have enough left for themselves. Other people have learned that it is fun to give and share things with others! Remember that God is always giving and generous in his love to all.

 Jesus himself said, "It is more blessed to give than to receive."
Acts 20:35 NIV

Give what little you have

One day Jesus watched the rich people give money at the temple. Then he saw a poor widow give the last two coins in her purse. Jesus explained that the widow was more generous with her small gift than all the others put together, because she was willing to give all the money she had. Read the story in *Luke 21:1-4*.

Give from the heart

You may feel that you have very little to give, but it's the way that you give that counts. If you give a gift because you think you have to, then it loses its value to others. Be thoughtful when you choose a present for someone and try to pick something that person would like. You can also be generous without spending any money. It costs nothing to share your time with others or give the small gift of a smile!

Share with those in need

One young boy was generous enough to share his lunch with the large crowd that had gathered to hear Jesus speak. The people were hungry, so the boy gave away his meal. He didn't think his five small loaves of bread and two fish would go very far. But when Jesus blessed the meal, an amazing thing happened. The disciples were able to feed the whole crowd, with twelve baskets of food left over! Read *John 6:1-14* to see how many people were in the crowd that day.

"I cleaned my sister's shoes for her because she didn't have time."
Matthew

Share whatever you have

When you are willing to be generous, even the smallest gifts can mean a lot. A short time spent explaining some schoolwork to a friend may be a big help when she does her homework. A loving hug from you when your dad gets home may cheer him up after a busy day at work. Share your love, time, and talents with others and see how much fun it is to spread happiness.

Be generous!

How can I be generous with my time?
- I can run an errand for my Dad.
- I can play a game that my sister likes.

How can I be generous with my talents?
- I can paint a picture to cheer up a friend who's sick.
- I can help my little brother with his homework.

How can I be generous with my things?
- I can share my toys when I play with my friends.
- I can give my old clothes to others who need them.

Dear Jesus,
I like to see people smile
when I give them something they like.
Thank you for showing me
how good it feels to give.
Help me to be generous every day.
Amen.
Annie

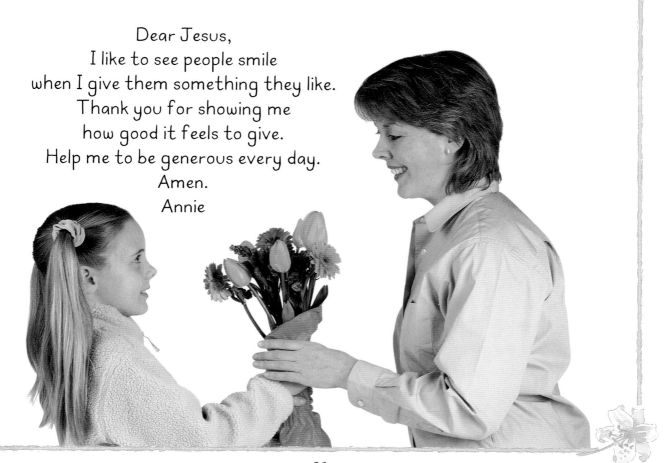

Patience

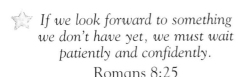

Having patience means waiting calmly for something without making a fuss. This could be raising your hand to answer a question in class, not interrupting when people are talking, or waiting your turn in a game. Being patient isn't always easy, but good things often come to those who wait!

If we look forward to something we don't have yet, we must wait patiently and confidently.
Romans 8:25

Don't be impatient!

Some things in life take time and can't be rushed. If you plant seeds in the garden, you will need to water the soil regularly and be prepared to wait. It might take days, even weeks, before your patience is rewarded and you see green shoots pushing up through the soil. It will take longer still for your seedlings to grow into large, healthy plants!

Worth the wait

Job was a very rich man who loved God with his whole heart. But in one day he lost everything: his home, his animals, all his servants, and even his children! And just when he thought things couldn't get any worse, he got painful sores all over his body. But Job continued to love and trust God. He patiently waited for God to help him, and God did! Find out how God rewarded Job's patience by reading *Job 42*.

Be patient!

How can I be patient at home?
- I can let my little sister get a drink before me.
- I can learn not to interrupt when others are talking.

How can I be patient with friends?
- I can take turns with my friends on the swings.
- I can let someone offer me a treat instead of asking for one.

I really don't like waiting, Lord.
It seems to take so long.
Show me how to be more patient
and enjoy the wait
as well as the rewards.
Amen.
Molly

Gratefulness

Gratefulness is being thankful and showing your appreciation to others when they do things for you. You can give a hug to someone who cares for you, thank a relative for a gift, or tell God you're grateful for the way he made you. Try to think of one thing to be grateful for every day.

Be grateful for life

Psalm 139 says, "You made all the delicate, inner parts of my body and knit them together in my mother's womb. Thank you for making me so wonderfully complex!" It is amazing to think about. Be grateful to God for making you one of a kind!

Be thankful

Just when Jonah was about to drown in the stormy sea, God sent a big fish to swallow him whole! Jonah was very grateful to God and told him so from inside the fish's belly. Later, when the fish spat him up onto dry land, Jonah showed how thankful he was by obeying God willingly. Find out what God asked Jonah to do by reading *Jonah 3*.

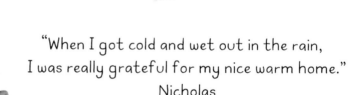

"When I got cold and wet out in the rain, I was really grateful for my nice warm home." Nicholas

Look on the bright side

Instead of feeling sorry for yourself when things go wrong, try to see something positive. *Romans 8:28* says that everything that happens to you can work out for your good if you love God. So no matter what is going on right now, you can be thankful to God for taking care of you.

Always say thank you

One day, Jesus visited a village where there were ten people suffering from a terrible skin disease called leprosy. The men begged Jesus to help them, so he made the leprosy go away. They all walked away completely well, but only one of them came back to thank Jesus. Read what Jesus had to say to the grateful man in *Luke 17:11-19*.

No matter what happens, always be thankful,
for this is God's will for you who belong to Christ Jesus.
1 Thessalonians 5:18 TLB

Appreciate what you have

It's easy to grumble and complain about all the things you want and forget to be grateful for the things you already have. When we are not grateful and content, we feel sad. Then we begin to feel sorry for ourselves. And this just makes us sadder. The way to feel better is to begin thinking about all the good things God has given us. Instead of wishing for what we don't have, we can be grateful for all we do have!

Be grateful!

How can I be grateful for my belongings?
- I can be grateful for my warm winter coat when it's cold.
- I can write a thank-you letter for a present I received.

How can I be grateful for my good health?
- I can be grateful for doctors and nurses, even when I need a shot.
- I can be thankful for my food, knowing there are many places where people don't have enough to eat.

How can I be grateful for other people?
- I can say thank you to my teacher for helping me learn.
- I can give thanks to God for my family and friends who love me.

Dear God,
I'm grateful that
I'm strong and healthy.
I'm thankful for
my family and friends.
Thank you for all the good
things you give me.
And thank you
for loving me!
Amen.
Lucy

Responsibility

Accepting responsibility means taking charge of the things you do for yourself and others. This could be brushing your teeth to keep them healthy, taking good care of a toy you borrow from a friend, or throwing your litter in the trash can to keep the park clean. If you show grown-ups that you can be trusted, they will let you have more responsibility.

You can handle it!

Taking on a new responsibility can be scary. You wonder if you'll be able to handle it. But tackling responsibilities is part of growing up.

Ask God to teach you to be responsible for your own actions. When you are crossing the street, remember to look both ways and listen for cars. Always cross where you can see and be seen. If you don't take responsibility for being careful around traffic, you or someone else could be hurt.

You're never too young

David was just a boy when he had the responsibility of looking after his family's flock of sheep. As a shepherd, he had to find fresh grass for the sheep, keep them safe from harm, and keep the flock together. You can read more about David in *1 Samuel 16*.

Looking after what's yours

If you own a pet, then it's your responsibility to look after it. Whether you have a dog, a cat, a rabbit, or a fish, your pet relies on you for its food and exercise. You need to take care of your pet every day of the year, not just when you feel like it.

Be sure to do what you should, for then you will enjoy the personal satisfaction of having done your work well.... For we are each responsible for our own conduct.
Galatians 6:4-5

A big responsibility

Noah accepted a great responsibility when God asked him to build a huge ark on dry land. This must have seemed like a strange thing to do, but Noah did everything exactly as God had commanded him. Once the ark was ready, Noah filled it with a male and female pair of every kind of bird and animal living on the earth. God trusted Noah to save all these animals from a mighty flood. Find out how the story ends in *Genesis 6-9*.

"Every weekend, I have to clean my room. Mom says it's my responsibility."
Emily

Earning trust

Your responsibilities may not seem as big as Noah's, but they are important. Doing what you are asked is another way of earning people's trust. Whether it's going to bed on time, or finishing your homework, think before you start complaining. If you do things without being asked or reminded, you'll prove to your mom and dad how responsible you can be!

Be responsible!

How can I be responsible for my health and body?

- I can wash my hands before meals.
- I can brush my hair to keep it neat.

How can I be responsible at home?

- I can put my dirty clothes in the laundry basket.
- I can put away my things after playing.

How can I be responsible for God's world?

- I can put food out for the wild birds in the winter.
- I can help recycle our household products.

Lord Jesus,
I lost my gloves today,
and Mom was upset with me.
She said I hadn't been
very responsible.
Sometimes responsibility
is hard to accept.
Please help me to take
better care
of all my things.
Amen.
James

Hard work

Doing hard work means making an effort to do your best at any task. It takes hard work to study for a test at school, write a thank-you note neatly, or help pull up all the weeds in the garden. If you are willing to work hard and get a lot done, you will feel happy to know you've done a job well. Remember that nothing worthwhile is ever achieved without hard work.

Take pride in your work

Don't be halfhearted and sloppy, because this shows that you don't care about your work. *Proverbs 21:5* says, "Good planning and hard work lead to prosperity, but hasty shortcuts lead to poverty." By making an extra effort to get a job done well, you will feel a sense of accomplishment, and God will be proud of you, too.

Make the effort

If something is important to you, then you should be prepared to work hard for it. Jesus told a story about what happened when a shepherd who cared about his sheep lost one of them. The shepherd spent all day and night searching for his sheep until he found it and returned it safely to the flock. You can read the story of the lost sheep in *Luke 15:4-7*.

Whatever you do, work at it with all your heart, as working for the Lord.
Colossians 3:23 NIV

Don't give up!

Learning to play a musical instrument or developing skill in a new sport takes lots of time and practice. When you have worked hard at something for awhile and don't see the results you'd hoped for, it can be difficult to keep going. Instead of getting discouraged, continue to work hard and do your best. Don't give up – your hard work will pay off eventually!

Work toward your goals

Whether they're big or small, it's important to have ambitions and dreams and to set goals for yourself. You might want to learn how to swim, or you might wish you were better at drawing. Whatever it is you are hoping to excel at, dream big and work hard. Most of all, remember that God is there to help you – so don't forget to ask him!

Take a break

Life shouldn't be all hard work. Everyone needs a rest from their efforts. When God made the world and everything in it, he worked hard for six days. On the seventh day God rested, because he'd finished his task. You can read the story of creation in *Genesis 1-2*.

"It took all day to build our tree house.
It was hard work helping Dad, but also lots of fun."
Rose

Be a hard worker!

How can I work hard at home?

- I can do my chores carefully, without rushing through them.
- I can turn off the television and help Mom when she's busy.

How can I work hard at school?

- I can do the work my teacher assigns for extra credit.
- I can study hard to learn the things that I find difficult.

How can I work hard at play?

- I can practice more to improve my sports skills.
- I can keep playing a game until it's finished.

Dear Jesus,
When I feel like rushing
through my schoolwork,
help me to take my time
and really study.
Help me to keep trying
until I succeed.
And thank you for times
of rest and play
when all the work is done!
Amen.
Rebecca

Honesty

Honesty means always telling the truth and doing what's right. Telling lies or cheating in games will only make you feel guilty and ashamed. Even if you get away with it, God knows when you are lying. Little lies can lead to bigger ones, and soon other people will not trust you. An honest person always tells the truth.

Unless you are honest in small matters,
you won't be in large ones.
If you cheat even a little, you won't
be honest with greater things.
Luke 16:10 TLB

Don't be tempted!

What would you do if you found someone's wallet in a parking lot? If no one was around, you might be tempted to help yourself to some of the money inside and leave the wallet where you found it. However, the honest thing to do would be to try and return the wallet to the person who lost it. Perhaps your honesty would be rewarded in some way by the thankful owner! Whatever the outcome, you would feel good about your decision to be honest.

A happier life

Zacchaeus was a tax collector who had grown rich by cheating people out of their money. Then one day he met Jesus and had a change of heart. Zacchaeus decided to give up his dishonest ways and pay back all the money he owed and more! By choosing to be honest, Zacchaeus became a happy man. Find out where Jesus first spoke to Zacchaeus by reading *Luke 19*.

Be honest!

How can I be honest in school?
- I can study hard and not cheat on tests.
- I can turn in things I find that others have lost.

How can I be honest with my friends and family?
- I can tell the truth when I break something by mistake.
- I can be honest with others about how I'm really feeling.

Dear God,
Today I did something wrong
and then told a lie
so I wouldn't get the blame.
Now I'm sorry that I wasn't honest.
Please help me to do the right thing
and tell the truth tomorrow.
Amen.
Alice

Bravery

Bravery means having the courage to face things that are scary or difficult. When you're brave, you trust God to help you stop being afraid of the dark, or worried about a hospital visit, or nervous about moving to a new town. Being brave may seem hard, but remember that God will always be with you, and he will help you. Just ask him!

Don't run away

Everyone gets scared at times – even grown-ups! But running away from something only means you have to face it later. When you are afraid, a brave thing to do is to share your worries with someone who loves Jesus. That person can pray with you and help turn a big problem into a small one.

Look fear in the face

David the shepherd boy acted bravely when he stood up against Goliath, a nine-foot-tall giant. David remembered how God had helped him kill a lion and a bear when he was protecting his flocks. So, instead of worrying that he was too small to fight Goliath, David took strength and courage from knowing that God was on his side. Find out what weapon David used to defeat Goliath in *1 Samuel 17:32-51*.

Learn to be bold

You, too, can be bold like David and choose to stand up to people who bully others. Bullies might seem to be brave, but deep down they're cowards. By having the courage to speak out for a friend who is being teased, you will help your friend, as well as earn the respect of others. Don't suffer in silence if you are being bullied at school. Always turn to a grown-up for help – and remember that God is with you, too.

For God did not give us a spirit of timidity, but a spirit of power, of love and of self-discipline.
2 Timothy 1:7 NIV

Speak out for others

God used Esther's bravery to save her people from death. She risked her own life by going to King Xerxes and asking for his protection against Haman, the man plotting to destroy her people. Instead of being angry, the king listened to what Esther had to say. Thanks to Esther's courage, the lives of many people were saved. Find out what happened to Esther's enemy by reading *Esther 7*.

"I stood up and sang
in front of the whole school today.
It was a little scary."
Rosie

Overcome your nerves

You may never have to speak to a king, but there will be times when you need to speak to someone who makes you feel nervous, like the school principal or the doctor. Or maybe you have a part in the school play and are scared because you have never acted in front of an audience before. Here's a good verse to remember from *Joshua 1:9* – "Be bold and strong! Banish fear and doubt! For remember, the Lord your God is with you wherever you go" (*TLB*).

Be brave!

How can I be brave at home?

- I can try not to whine when I hurt myself or feel ill.
- I can tell Mom or Dad when I'm afraid of something.

How can I be brave at school?

- I can stand up to a classmate who is teasing me.
- I can try out for a part in the school play.

How can I be brave away from home?

- I can smile at the dentist and not make a fuss.
- I can sleep over at a friend's house and not be scared.

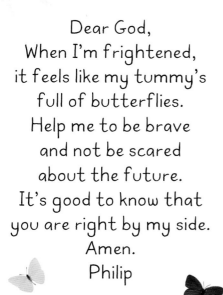

Dear God,
When I'm frightened,
it feels like my tummy's
full of butterflies.
Help me to be brave
and not be scared
about the future.
It's good to know that
you are right by my side.
Amen.
Philip

Faithfulness

Faithfulness means being loyal and true in your words and actions toward others and toward God. When you keep a promise you have made, or are on time for a meeting, you are showing people that you can be relied upon. Faithful friends are close friends who look out for one another.

Keep your word

Try to keep your promises to others so your friends and family will keep on trusting you. People feel let down and disappointed by those who don't keep their word. Remember that God always keeps his word. The Bible says in *Lamentations 3:23* – "Great is his faithfulness; his loving kindness begins afresh each day" (*TLB*).

"My friend Sam and I go everywhere together – we're faithful friends."
William

Stay true

King Darius punished Daniel for staying faithful to God. When Daniel refused to stop praying, the king locked him up in a den of hungry lions. During the night, God came to Daniel's rescue and kept him safe from harm. Read *Daniel 6* to find out what happened when King Darius found Daniel alive the next morning.

Be faithful!

How can I be faithful to my friends?

- I can show up for band practice every week.
- I can be there for my best friend when she needs my support.

How can I be faithful to my family?

- I can remember to do the chores that I agreed to do.
- I can keep my promise to take care of my brother.

Dear Lord,
Thank you for always being there
when we need you.
Thank you for keeping
the promises that you made to us.
Help me follow your example
and be faithful to others.
Amen.
Danni

Joyfulness

Joyfulness means knowing that you are loved by God and free to enjoy life. Rolling down a grassy hill on a summer's day, celebrating a good friend's birthday, and being glad you're alive are all ways to show joyfulness. Joyfulness begins deep inside of you, and spills out to the people around you. Joy is more than just a feeling – it's a gift to be shared with others.

Joy keeps you strong

There's a difference between joyfulness and happiness. When everything is going the way you want, you feel happy. But when you trust God, you can be joyful even when things aren't going well. Joy comes from being confident and secure in God's love and care, no matter how bad things might seem. Remember this verse from *Nehemiah 8:10* – "The joy of the Lord is your strength."

I know the Lord is always with me.
No wonder my heart is filled with joy!
Psalm 16:8-9

Sing joyfully

God parted the waters of the Red Sea so that Moses and the Israelite slaves could escape from Egypt. Once they had safely crossed to the other side of the sea, the Israelites realized that they were free at last! Miriam was so full of joy that she started to dance and sing. Read *Exodus 15:20* to find out which instrument Miriam played as she sang her praise to God.

Be joyful!

How can I be joyful at home?

- I can enjoy spending time with my family.
- I can express my joy by singing while I do my chores.

How can I be joyful at school?

- I can cheer up my friends when they're feeling down.
- I can smile at my teachers as I come into class.

Dear God,
I am full of joy because you love me!
No matter what happens,
I know you will take care of me.
Help me to share my joyfulness
with everyone I know.
Amen.
Caroline

Index of Bible verses

Acknowledgments

Unless otherwise indicated, all Scripture quotations are taken from the *Holy Bible*, New Living Translation, copyright © 1996. Used by permission of Tyndale House Publishers, Inc., Wheaton, Illinois 60189. All rights reserved.

Scripture verses marked TLB are taken from *The Living Bible*, copyright © 1971 owned by assignment by KNT Charitable Trust. All rights reserved.

Scripture quotations marked NIV are taken from the *Holy Bible*, New International Version (r). Copyright © 1973, 1978, 1984 by International Bible Society. Used by permission of Zondervan Publishing House. All rights reserved.

The author would like to thank the children, teachers, and parents of Great Gaddesden School, Hertfordshire, England, for their thoughts on values. Thanks also to all those who have listened to many outlines over numerous cups of coffee – your value is beyond worth.

Dorling Kindersley would like to thank the following people for appearing in this book: Yolanda Batson, Reece Beckles, Tobias Briscoe, Sophie Bunten, Penny Canning, Karanveer Chankana, Georgina Chenery, George Gee, Peter Kelleher, Dawn Sirett, Phoebe Sirett Harrison, Joseph Terashina, Lily Terashina, Oscar Wilkins, Danielle Wright, Lesley Wright.

The publisher would like to thank the following for their kind permission to reproduce their photographs: b=bottom, l=left
Corbis UK Ltd: 33; **Pictor International:** 17; **The Stock Market:** Front Jacket; **Tony Stone Images:** Pascal Crapet 30; **Telegraph Colour Library:** 18b, 19, 20b; R Chapple 25bl; J Cummins 16, 26b, 34b; Robin Davies 40; Jean-Francois Humbert 11b; R Goldman 46b; A Tilley 12b.

Additional photography by Paul Bricknell, Andy Crawford, Jo Foord, Steve Gorton, Frank Greenaway, Derek Hall, Colin Keates, Dave King, Natural History Museum, Ian O'Leary, Stephen Oliver, Susanna Price, Tim Ridley, Steve Shott, Matthew Ward.